MW01492033

GIRLS GUIDE:
HOW TO BE A SISTER ©

Angela D. Coleman, MBA, CNM

sisterhoodagenda.com

First published in 2015
By Sisterhood Agenda Enterprises, LLC

Sisterhood Agenda Enterprises, LLC
Girls Guide: How to Be a Sister

ISBN-13: 978-0-9916565-4-7

Edited by Nancy Danch.

Cover design by Kelsey Leigh.

Back cover photograph by Eliza Magro.

Printed in the United States of America.

GIRLS GUIDE:
HOW TO BE A SISTER©

CELEBRATING 20 YEARS
OF SISTERHOOD

With the Sisterhood Manifesto by Blanche Williams

Introduction

It's hard to believe that it's been 20 years since I started Sisterhood Agenda! Unlike many national social service agencies, Sisterhood Agenda is much different today than when we first started.

In 1994, Sisterhood Agenda was started on the principle that the spirit of sisterhood must be the foundation of any women's empowerment movement. From my thesis work, stigmatization, and ethnic identity labels, I knew that "African American" did not include all sisters. Our target population was women and girls of African descent serving all ages, with youth as our primary focus.

When the Internet became available for public use (yes, I am letting you know just how old I really am!), an online search for "Black woman" resulted in pages and pages of pornography. Still, today, those same Internet searches contain pornography, but, importantly, they also show us the multitude of women organizations, websites, and resources for Black females.

Fast forward to now, 2015, things are different. I soon discovered our sisterhood must include ALL women because our common interests greatly outnumber our differences. Isn't that what sisterhood is all about?

The spirit of sisterhood has taken on a more endearing presence. Sisterhood does not consist of just one ethnic group; it is a global movement that includes women and girls from every culture and from all different geographic locations throughout the world. Yes, sisterhood still holds true as the foundation of any women's movement!

Most of us assume that we know what it means to be a sister. If this were the case, the world would be a much better place. Like most values, sisterhood must be taught and when the foundation is set, it must be practiced daily. The spirit of sisterhood permeates all aspects of our lives. We can and should be sisters because sisterhood empowers each other and the world.

In the Spirit of Sisterhood,

Angela D. Coleman

WHAT IS A SISTER?

"A sister is a gift to the heart, a friend to the spirit, a golden thread to the meaning of life."
Isadora James

Some say that a sister is a forever friend.

Every so often, something beautiful happens - a woman shows another woman love. This is not love based on any type of physical attraction, but love based on honest commitment, a sense of caring, devotion, and tenderness. What should be a common occurrence sometimes constitutes a miracle due to its rare manifestation.

Over the years, I have learned a lot about sisterhood; mainly that it cannot be judged on a superficial level.
It would be nice if every woman was a sister; however, this is not the case. This realization often breeds distrust

among us. Nonetheless, instead of being standoffish, we can be wise.

To empower ourselves individually and collectively we must first recognize who is on our sister-team and who is an enemy. We must keep in mind the fact that the enemy is often disguised as a sister-friend. We must choose our female company with high standards and specific guidelines. It is not easy, but this awareness can prevent a lot of disappointment based on failed expectations.

What is a sister? What do they do, who are they, and where can I find one? A sister is called a sister because the term implies a bond so strong that it is like that of a blood relative. Sisterhood is the warmth and familiarity of family. A sister is someone who always has your back and can tell you the truth about yourself. She is someone who can assist you in all aspects of your self-development, even if your goals, aspirations, and accomplishments exceed her own. She is not jealous of you, but feels like your victory is also her victory because she wants the best for you. She knows that you will share your joy and material wealth with her. Always remember that sisterhood is a privilege, not a right. In this sense, biological sisters are not automatically sisters because it is the spirit that counts, not the lineage. If you have to ask yourself if someone is your sister, chances are, she is not.

Sisters can be found anywhere since we populate the world, but all prejudices must first be eradicated. As with all powerful relationships, we must get ourselves together first before we can interact healthfully with others. Before you judge other females according to physical appearances, incomes, or regional differences, know that the divine exists in everyone and everything.

Our struggles have left scars on our psyches and in our lives, passed down from generation to generation. When we do not love ourselves as women, we cannot smile, compliment, and be kind to other women. When we do not have confidence in our futures, we negate the success of others and secretly desire what they have. When we do not recognize our own natural beauty, we become dependent upon superficial things and external relationships to validate our personal worth. This, unhealthy dependence will eventually cause us to treat ourselves, and those around us, in an "unsisterly" manner.

Sisterhood is a largely untapped force, a kinship so strong it can threaten the status quo. Transcending superficial boundaries of beauty, class, and sometimes, race, the power remains more potential than actual because we often do not recognize our magical greatness. Before you point fingers at her, look at yourself.

Are you the best sister that you can be? Are you open to developing real relationships with other females based on mutual respect, admiration, love, and trust? Do you treat others as you want and expect to be treated? Only when you are a sister yourself can you define, identify, and bond with other sisters. Only then can we be the positive, life-altering force that can change what we know as reality to positively affect the world.

What You Can Do:
- *Think about what sisterhood means to you. Do you agree or disagree with my definition of a sister? What would you add or change?*

- *Think about how you feel when you are around other women. Is it a different feeling when you spend time with women of different ethnicities? What makes it different?*

- *Think about what it means to be a positive sister and whether or not you fit this description. How can you be a great sister?*

OUR ACTIONS
"There is a special place in hell for women
who don't help other women."
Madeleine Albright

There is an assumption that all women stick together. We know this is simply not true. It would be great if we hail total strangers on the street, smile, and keep our positive vibes moving, woman-to-woman, and some of us really do try.

The diversity of our sisterhood is AMAZING!

On Princeton University's campus, I was one of a very small percentage of African Americans (less than 3%). When I saw other Black people, I instantly felt a kinship with them. They were familiar to me, like my neighborhood, even my family. This type of instant connection is something that non-Black people tend to question, even be envious of. Some may even call it racist. However, at this place and time, I did not feel the love. On this Ivy League campus in the 1990's, the feeling was rarely reciprocated. They looked at me like I was crazy, like, "Do I know you?" We understand now that being a sister is not biological.

Sisterhood is about our actions, feelings, and behavior, it should become clear that anyone (male, female, Black, White, Asian, Indian, European, etc.) has the potential to be a sister. In fact, men can put sisterhood on their agendas, too! This definition and acceptance is the polar opposite of any sexism, racist intention, or action.

If you ever have a doubt, look below. Here is a clear chart about actions that constitute sisterly behavior and those that do not:

SISTER BEHAVIOR	NON- SISTER BEHAVIOR
Provides unconditional love, consistently	Gives you loving attention only when she needs something from you
Is affectionate when appropriate	Refuses to show affection due to fear of looking "gay"
Makes time for you when you need it; she will always be there	Asks you for help when she needs it but is often too busy when you need her help
Helps you succeed in your job by giving you resources and encouragement	Competes with you on and off the job; will not offer you a hand-up or mentor you because she thinks there can

	only be one allowed to succeed and she is the one
Provides helpful advice with your personal relationships; the advice has your happiness at its foundation	Secretly feels good when your personal relationships suffer; misery loves company and she is threatened by your happiness
Teaches young girls how to be sisters	Teaches young girls how to distrust and hate each other
Encourages different points of view; welcomes and appreciates a diverse sisterhood	Has limited visions of reality; discourages other opinions, ways of thinking, doing, and existing
Understands and knows how to share power	Holds on to her limited power out of fear
Understands that when we support each other as females, we all do better	Does not know how to support other women and lacks the desire to learn
Is comfortable with her friends, boyfriend, and family members around each other and around other women	Women make her suspicious and nervous; she avoids group gatherings and tends to relate to each person individually
Is very comfortable complimenting other girls and women, likes to acknowledge their strengths	Is extremely threatened by other women and girls, especially if they are young, smart, and attractive; smiles in their faces and talks about them behind their back
Sees sisterhood across	Does not identify with other

class lines, racial, and geographic barriers	females who have less than she does; separates herself from girls who are "ghetto," economically disenfranchised, lacking proper etiquette, or residing in different communities because she believes that she is superior to them
Accepts differences in culture without inferiority/superiority judgments; she aspires to be like her royal ancient ancestors	Aspires to be as European as possible; believes that White is right; negates the Motherland and foreign cultures believing they are "primitive"
Is inspired to act in ways that make herself and her sisterhood collective look and feel good	Has an "everybody for themselves" mentality where her primary concern is herself
Will tell you when there is something on the back of your skirt	Will stare at it and tell someone else so that they can laugh together
Willingly gives you her bed to sleep in when you need it	Suggests a hotel or other sleeping arrangement due to the "inconvenience"
Sees you struggling and offers assistance	Sees you struggling and does nothing to help
Has leadership potential and abilities; uses her own mind to make decisions	Consistently looks for someone to follow; only knows and follows popular culture and trends

What You Can Do:

- *Identify the sisters and non-sisters in your life. Engage with the sisters and disengage from the non-sisters.*

- *Make a list of at least five additional things that sisters do.*

- *Do you do what sisters do? Why or why not?*

WHY SISTERHOOD MATTERS

"Any woman who chooses to behave like a full human being should be warned that the armies of the status quo will treat her as something of a dirty joke . . . She will need her sisterhood."
Gloria Steinem

On her website, www.legaci.com, blogger Jessica Ann Mitchell writes:

"To share your story... To be real with a circle of people you can trust, is one of the best feelings in the world. And I deeply believe that it is through these types of bonds that Black women have been able to survive so many atrocities and still come out with our sanity. Safe spaces in the presence of our sisters is the place to heal because we know so much of the world seems against us, rushes to judge us, and disregards our truth. It was in these moments that I felt a wholeness that can only be achieved in knowing that these sisters had my back. We could go to each other for anything..."

Bonding with your sisters is a natural phenomenon.

This story about sister support and encouragement resonates with many women, not just Black women. To bond and connect in such a meaningful way is not a fantasy, but can be our reality. The benefits that will come our way are numerous. We need to unite in sisterhood so that we empower each other.

When you empower women, you empower the entire community. Hence, there is no community empowerment without women's empowerment. Historically, our female ancestors have controlled the economy of the marketplace and have played a substantial part in the buying and selling of services.

From the manufacturing of food, to the creation of clothing and other textiles, it is through our hands that innovation, creativity, sustainability, and currency has been and is exchanged. This fact holds true today in many communities throughout the world including those in Africa, Asia, and India. Of course, women warriors are also a historical fact.

Warrior sisters from Benin: beautiful, cultural, and dangerous!
Meschac Gaba's Museum of Contemporary African Art

William Moulton Marston, an American psychologist and writer who was already famous for inventing the polygraph (forerunner to Wonder Woman's magic lasso), struck upon an idea for a new kind of superhero, one who would triumph not with fists or firepower, but with love. "Fine," said Elizabeth, his wife. "But make her a woman."

The superhero that Marston created became known as Wonder Woman. We can look at Wonder Woman as an archetype of female empowerment. In the comics and also in an older television series, Wonder Woman is portrayed as a superheroine. Created by Marston and published by DC Comics, Wonder Woman fights for justice, love, peace, and gender equality. Wonder Woman is a warrior princess of the Amazons tribe, native to Paradise Island, a secluded island in the middle of a vast ocean. In her homeland, Wonder Woman is a Princess, known as Princess Diana of Themyscira.

When Captain Steve Trevor crash-landed on their island, Diana's mother, Hippolyte, Queen of the Amazons, held a competition to find the most worthy of all the women. The winner, her daughter Diana in disguise, had the responsibility to take Captain Steve Trevor back to the man's world and fight for justice. Diana Prince was Wonder Woman's secret identity. Wonder Woman is gifted with a wide range of superhuman powers along with superior combat and battle skills. She possesses an arsenal of weapons which include the Lasso of Truth, a pair of indestructible bracelets, a tiara which serves as a projectile, and, in some stories, an invisible airplane.

Marston wrote in 1943, "Wonder Woman is psychological propaganda for the new type of woman who should, I believe, rule the world." Further, in a 1943 issue of *The American Scholar*, Marston wrote:

"Not even girls want to be girls so long as our feminine archetype lacks force, strength, and power. Not wanting to be girls, they don't want to be tender, submissive, peace-loving as good women are. Women's strong qualities have become despised because of their weakness. The obvious remedy is to create a feminine character with all the strength of Superman plus all the allure of a good and beautiful woman."

Photo credit: Wonder Woman is a creation of DC Comics.

A little-known fact: Nubia was Wonder Woman's Black sister, created from black clay, just as Diana was created from white clay. Like Diana, Nubia, appearing in almost twenty DC Comics issues, has superhuman strength. Nubia also possessed a magic sword, the only weapon on Earth that could counteract Diana's magic lasso. She could also glide on air currents. Nubia's magical armor with a raised embossed lion's head on its breastplate enabled her to time travel to mystical realms. Diana and Nubia universally transcend human limitations through wisdom, knowledge, and use of natural forces for good such as her sun energy shield and chest emblem.

Sisterhood matters because we need more women like Wonder Woman and Nubia. We all have the capacity to be them with a collective responsibility to promote justice, love, peace, gender AND racial equality. Our sisterhood is a tribe and each of us is gifted with something unique, our own arsenal of knowledge, skills, and weapons (not literally, but figuratively) to assist us in our mission. Our tribe is a diverse sisterhood exemplified in the many shapes, colors, and textures of our physical selves.

In this world of fiction, the Amazons are a healthy matriarchal tribe. Some of them have titles, they have competitions, but they are simultaneously able to respect, care for, and co-exist with men. The women are beautiful, talented, and powerful. Nevertheless, why does this world have to be fictitious? We have to see this vision and want this type of sisterhood to be a reality for us and our families. It does not exist in a vacuum since we do not all live on a secluded island of women in the middle of the ocean. However, with sisterhood, we can manifest this reality of empowered femininity within our communities.

What You Can Do:
- *Are you a wonder woman? Do you have a secret identity? What are your powers?*

- *Do you have a tribe? Identify the characteristics of your tribe.*

- *Have you ever envisioned superheroes of other ethnicities? Why or why not?*

WOMEN'S EMPOWERMENT

"The spirit of sisterhood must be the foundation of any women's empowerment movement."
Angela D. Coleman

In times of hardship and despair, we have historically come together and supported each other as sisters. But when does this sisterhood become empowerment?

We battled and rallied side by side. When one wins, we all win.

I constantly see women's empowerment activities taking place throughout many U.S. cities. Often, a radio station conglomerate sponsors the larger events and the smaller ones are sponsored by community-based organizations. Some target adults only while others include activities for girls. Some even include the "fellas" in their agenda. The women's empowerment activities can be both for-profit and non-profit.

Whether you have celebrity keynote speakers and lots of promotion or not, you can learn a lot or you can learn a little. What they all have in common is that they are trying to draw you in. There is no women's empowerment without women. At these important gathering opportunities, are we setting the agenda and getting what we really need?

What happens when women come together? Without sisterhood on the agenda, there are severe limitations to the process. I've said it before and I will say it again: The spirit of sisterhood must be a part of any women's empowerment movement; we must establish the foundation so that the real work can begin.

Many women's empowerment programs operate on the assumption that we are at a healthier, often higher, level of functioning than we actually are. This is a mistake if we truly want to empower those who participate. Most women are

NOT operating on the principles of sisterhood and must be instructed on how to do so.

Women empowerment programs are the perfect opportunity to help women and girls practice sisterhood, feel the effects of its processes, and cultivate its power. When sisterhood is not on the agenda, it is a missed opportunity for individual and collective growth.

In the spirit of sisterhood, we can be united in our quest for freedom.

When women empowerment activities focus on business, health, girls, or other self-development, what we are trying to create? Whether we call it this or not, it is most definitely sisterhood. The foundation is the same. For one to truly begin the empowerment process, it is necessary to be able to address the foundation first by helping participants raise their level of sisterhood.

What is empowerment, anyway? We hear about it all the time and read about it constantly. Empowerment may mean different things to different people, but there are initial key elements to the empowerment process.

Empowerment instills knowledge, self-awareness, and hope. Empowerment is a process by which people, organizations, and communities gain mastery over issues of concern to them. Efforts to gain control, access to resources, and a critical understanding of one's sociopolitical context are fundamental aspects of empowerment processes.

Separately and distinctly, there are individual, group, and community empowerment processes. All empowerment must have an impact at the individual level. This is intuitive because groups and communities are comprised of individuals. However, the dynamics of empowerment on individual, group, and community levels are different. For example, on a personal level, being a member of an empowered group can help me become empowered as an individual. Hence, I do not have to begin as an empowered person—I can transform into it by association.

We need it ALL to be powerful. Access is especially important, as we have historically been blocked from the valuable resources necessary to progress. Today, we have learned to use our creativity to surmount these obstacles and avoid becoming a marginalized and disenfranchised statistic.

What empowers individuals? What empowers groups and communities? It is CONSCIOUSNESS. Consciousness is defined as "the state of being awake and aware of one's surroundings, awareness, or perception by the mind of itself and the world." Sisterhood Agenda and other sisterhood movement organizations empower their female constituents by increasing consciousness about issues that we care about.

In Sisterhood Agenda's empowerment workshops, we taught and explained the organization's Power Equation:

Self-Knowledge + Self-Development + Self-Esteem
=CONSCIOUSNESS → EMPOWERMENT

Again, this is empowerment on the individual level where self-knowledge, self-development, and self-esteem combine to raise consciousness, sometimes to the level of enlightenment, moving us out of the dark and into the light. Enlightenment: the action or state of attaining or having attained spiritual knowledge or insight, in particular, that awareness which frees a person.

However, it is not okay to just "know." The knowledge has to actually be used to gain mastery over issues of concern to that individual. Therefore, this consciousness (gained through self-knowledge, self-development, and self-esteem) will only result in true empowerment when it is transformed into action.

When you add "Sisterhood" to the equation, you can achieve empowerment on group and community levels because consciousness-raising tools and techniques are shared in the spirit of sisterhood, certainly the most powerful empowerment tool for female empowerment:

Sisterhood
+ Self-Knowledge
+ Self-Development
+ Self-Esteem
=CONSCIOUSNESS → EMPOWERMENT

Thus, using the power of sisterhood, we can empower entire groups and communities through consciousness-raising activities (self-knowledge, self-development, and self-esteem). Keeping in mind, just as with individual empowerment processes, conscious sisters must COLLECTIVELY use their knowledge to gain mastery over issues of concern to the group. We have to actually transform our collective consciousness into collective action to empower the group as a whole.

Similar to individual empowerment processes, collective consciousness-raising can rise to the level of collective enlightenment. When collective consciousness is transformed into collective action, collective empowerment results. This is why true empowerment among groups of women is more rare than we might realize.

When consciousness leads to action and transcends to enlightenment, sisterhood becomes more than women sitting around supporting each other. Enlightenment on group and community levels strengthens the whole and often leads to MOVEMENTS. Movements are defined as prevalent thinking and widespread action that results in long-lasting, often permanent positive social change. That is why there can be no women's empowerment movement without sisterhood.

Along with all of the resources that I could access at the time, I created the Power Equation when I was 23-years old. The Power Equation is still alive and fully functioning today as Sisterhood Agenda's four empowerment principles: sisterhood, self-knowledge, self-development, and self-esteem.

We could look at our historical movements in the past and see where the Power Equation and our empowerment movements manifested themselves for positive social change. Shirley Chisholm for President, Wilma Mankiller as Chief of the Cherokee Nation, the feminist movement, the womanist movement, Hillary Clinton for President, global natural hair movement, and the global sisterhood movement (of course!) are just a few examples.

What You Can Do:

- *Think of yourself as an empowered individual. What are you doing everyday?*

- *Think of five ways to make women empowerment conferences more effective. How can you make this happen in your community?*

- *Track the sisterhood movement in your community. What do you see?*

WHERE IS THE SISTERHOOD?

I don't believe an accident of birth makes people sisters or brothers. It makes them siblings, gives them mutuality of parentage. Sisterhood and brotherhood is a condition people have to work at."
Maya Angelou

When I travel to different places, I can immediately sense whether the sisterhood is there or if it is not. More often than not, there is a diverse, mixed group. There are varying degrees of awareness and their response to my work and to me is very revealing. No matter the locale, this fact remains the same: the biggest obstacle to sisterhood is an unconscious sister.

When a sister is unconscious, she is consciously or inadvertently, trying to bring you down. Because she is trying to bring you down, this further proves the point that this unconscious sister is really beneath you. An unconscious sister is one who does not understand her worth, her heritage, or the global significance of her place in the world as a woman. She complains, blames, and competes instead of working on herself and working together with others. She is more comfortable being identified as spiteful or overbearing rather than being identified as a queen.

For many sisters, there is often a strong disconnect between us because we have been taught to be detached and separated, especially between different ethnic groups. When stereotypes are promoted in media and we are attacked by people who don't understand or respect us, anger and mistrust are the result. Another unfortunate result is that, too often, we end up attacking each other. The ugly head of negativity can prove powerful by prompting us to destroy each other publicly and privately rather than to try and connect through our sisterhood bond, shared experiences, and the power of our united womanhood.

These unconscious sisters do not recognize the gender, cultural, social, economic, and health disparities that exist because they do not see themselves as part of a larger collective. As far as this unconscious sister is concerned, her issues are unique to her and also add in the fact that she has few true friends, if any at all. She doesn't like, trust, or respect other women; she must be very lonely.

When I am around these types of sisters, I tend to put up a protective shield that fortifies me. I don't want their energy to get mixed up with my own because I don't want it to taint me and influence me to think and behave the way that they do. I have to do this so that they won't psyche me out and throw me off of my game. Unfortunately, in many of my travels, I see this behavior and it crosses many borders.

The simple and effective tactic of divide and conquer is alive and well. Too many sisters identify with their race, ethnicity, tribe, country, or nation instead of their very invaluable part of our entire woman collective. As we compete with each other and tell ourselves who is better than whom, our identity, our families, our economic freedom, and our territories are slipping away from us.

"The solution is not for women to stop doing what we do. The solution is to make our communities places that accept us for being ourselves."

—Shahd Majeed

Sisterhood, in its wholeness, is a beautiful thing, but terrifying for a patriarchal society where the status quo keeps women and girls marginalized, without resources and assets to build. Building is what we must do, not just to prosper, but also to survive. To build sisterhood, we must seek and unite with similar others. Where can we go for sisterhood?

Unity in sisterhood is a magnificent sight to behold.

I go to my closest and best allies who understand me. These are the sisters that recognize how I defy labels and stereotypes. My sisterhood includes those who support my mission-driven work with Sisterhood Agenda and those who respect me as a woman. My sisterhood includes women of different ethnicities. My sisterhood includes members of my biological family, bonded friends, and a few significant others. Most importantly, my sisterhood defies all geographic boundaries; my sisterhood includes over 3,500 agencies, their leaders, staff, and constituents who also GET IT—they understand and believe in the power of sisterhood. They are the Sisterhood Agenda global partners in 34 countries who say, yes, women are important and our issues need to be addressed.

However, I can't completely ignore the unconscious sisters, either. Increasing sisterhood consciousness and enlightenment among sisters in the dark is my biggest challenge and one that I have accepted as part of my life's work. One of my goals in life is to spread sister consciousness and love to everyone I come into contact with, whether they recognize it or not. "Conversion" is not necessary, nor is it required.

Spreading sister consciousness and love when media promotes anti-sisterhood propaganda is not easy. Too often, from a very young age, we are taught to compete with other girls, hate, and fight each other. Who is teaching us these fallacies and why do we believe it? When will we stop entertaining them and focus on building ourselves?

I encourage you to develop yourself, increase your sisterhood consciousness, and find like-minded others. In other words, find and develop your sisterhood, making sure to surround yourself with those who can help you.

What You Can Do:
- *List at least three places to get your sisterhood.*

- *Anti-sisterhood media is popular. List specific ways to counteract it.*

- *Think of three women who are non-sisters. How can you help non-sisters become sisters?*

SISTERHOOD MANIFESTO
"We are our sisters. Stay committed to keeping each other company, keeping each other smiling, and keeping each other conscious."
Blanche Williams

The 21st Century is about technology, progress, and social change. Collaboration is the buzzword and our sense of global community is greatly enhanced.

Blanche Williams, founder of the National Black Women's Town Hall, created the 21st Century Sisterhood of Greatness Manifesto to encourage women to reclaim their magnificence by manifesting the power and beauty of sisterhood in the new millennium.

Her manifesto is an excellent model for group empowerment and gives us a reference that we can all utilize everyday.

From the language, you can clearly see that it is a 10-step call to action, thereby, inspiring the sisterhood movement. A timely document, here it is, reprinted with permission:

1. Redefine Our Identity
Redefine our identity by consciously rejecting the unhealthy, untrue, and unworthy images that attempt to deny our greatness, extinguish our brilliance, and defeat our spirit. We instead stand firmly in our divine birthright to live a life adorned with grace, excellence, and integrity. We will align ourselves with like-minds and assign our goals with like-achievers.

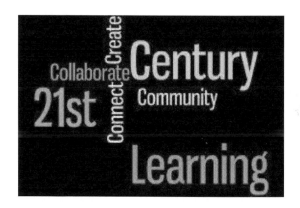

2. Reclaim Our Dignity
Reclaim our dignity by walking in the spirit of decency and humility regardless of images that show less than our finest. We will embrace and face that which pierces our dignity as women and girls, in order to recognize and reshape its effect on our thoughts and expressions. We will no longer allow external forces to dictate the choices we make or the actions

we take but will empower our intuitive intelligence to be the force that guides us. We are sisters first, regardless of the diversity of life and styles we encompass.

3. Revolutionize Our Thinking

Revolutionize our thinking by being willing to step outside our box of boundaries and self-imposed limitations. We will develop a willingness to break down the walls of negativity, doubt, fear, and jealousy to rebuild a mindset strong, positive, and forward thinking. We will shatter our mind's glass ceiling and learn to soar above the frays of mediocrity. Our evolution as women must be televised in order to demystify those images that have been allowed to run rampant throughout our society.

4. Redesign Our Image

Redesign our image by reshaping and remolding ourselves into who we want to represent instead of what sells. We will learn to take the front seat to frame who we are and not the back seat and take what others want us to emulate. We will learn to take the high road where our ancestors taught us we should be and not the low road where we "dummy down" and accept being marginalized, objectified or hypersexualized. We will speak out and up for ourselves and our sisters when anyone attempts to disrespect our legacies. We will chart a course that will illuminate our diversity, celebrate our fabulosity, and stimulate our ambitions. We will be the architects of our destiny and builders of our endless possibilities.

5. Rebirth Our Self-Respect

Rebirth our self-respect by understanding and accepting that we are endowed with the right to be respected, revered, honored and adored. As women, we raise the children. As women, we adorn the heavens with the spirits of queens, sojourners, leaders, mothers, daughters and friends. As women, we birth the spirits that knock at our doors of consciousness. As we grow in the ways of sisterhood, we will learn to rebirth a nation that begins within the womb of our feelings, our self-worth, and our self-love. The sisterhood can only give what it possesses, therefore we are committed to nurture, support, and uplift the inner child in us all. We will show loving respect for every sister as we grow to fully and authentically love and respect ourselves.

6. Rebuild Our Relationships

Rebuild our relationships by being accountable for who we are and the role we play in the lives of others. Are our bonds breakable or unshakeable? We will learn to thoughtfully explore the connections we have with other women and girls and express how much we honor their presence in our lives. Are there sister relationships that need re-energizing or do you need a personal overhaul to re-evaluate, re-access or re-focus yourself? Do we treat or speak about our sisters with venom or encourage them to victory? The sisterhood will not tolerate cheating on the spirit of a sister through jealousy, deceit, or defamation of character. Learn to let people be who they are and turn your focus inward by making a personal pledge to live up to your destiny of greatness; mind, body, spirit, and deeds.

7. Restore Our Hope

Restore our hope by each sister living their dreams. We can't allow anyone's image or descriptions of us diminish our goal and date with destiny. The best revenge is performance. As we align together in force and focus, we will be the hope and the dream of our ancestors who put the "p" in purpose, pride, and perseverance. We didn't struggle and stride to now lose our sense of direction. Regardless of what you see, we know better and we must do better to hold each other accountable. Together we can be rock solid in our dedication to uphold the code of the Sisterhood of Greatness.

8. Reconnect With Our Body

Reconnect with the vessel that houses the greatness that lives within by releasing self-judgment, negative and neglectful thoughts. We are charged with reverencing, maintaining, and embracing our bodies by integrating positive habits that encourage a healthy life and spirit of wellness. The way we treat and care for ourselves is a direct reflection of how we perceive our self-worth. Our bodies are sacred and hold a divine connection with our inner being and outer humanity.

9. Redeem Our Soulful Spirit

Redeem our soulful spirits by unleashing the false perceptions and conceptions we have about ourselves and our ability to rise above adversity to live in peace and harmony. We are designed to be mindfully innovative, to excel at all things, and to love and be loved in abundance. God's universe awaits our instruction and bows to our every wish and desire. We must learn to work through our doubts and fears in order to truly reach our highest potential.

10. Re-Unite Our Sisterhood

Re-unite our sisterhood by coming together. Bring someone extra to the table. We are tied to each other because of the fabric we were created within. Our roles are interchangeable because our maturation is tied to diversity of experience, exposure, and insight. Our power is intergenerational!

When we look at the landscape of our lives, there will always be a sister who can help you through any peak or valley because they have already walked that path. We will learn to be each other's source and voice. When we apply our understanding and willingness to tap into the wisdom of the sisterhood we will experience a bond that is transformative and exhilarating. We are our sisters. Stay committed to keeping each other company, keeping each other smiling, and keeping
each other conscious.

What You Can Do:
- *Read one step of the Sisterhood Manifesto everyday to reinforce your commitment to sisterhood.*

- *Add your own step to the manifesto. What else do you think we should do as sisters?*

- *Focus on step #10: Re-Unite Our Sisterhood. Make sure you invite someone into your sisterhood this week.*

THE FUTURE OF SISTERHOOD

"Women are going to form a chain, a greater sisterhood than the world has ever known."
Nellie L. McClung

Sisterhood used to be localized, but with today's technology and expansive reach, sisterhood is global. Women populate the world in even the most remote and obscure geographic locations. Furthermore, from every location with technology access, we can be sisters.

Now and in the future, our femininity (or female-ness) binds our sisterhood. Our gender is an opportunity to create a sisterhood that binds us by blood, biology, and culture. It is a tribe unlike any other.

Because our cultural identity can be so strong, I believe that the future of sisterhood explicitly acknowledges our cultural significance. Culture is a learning tool, a way to share our more intimate selves with others. This allows us to build upon our shared cultural values, including, but not limited to, our historical memory of unity, harmony with nature, and special gifts.

Did you notice? We are evolving into new eras of consciousness with our sisterhood. We are beginning to expect and require more from ourselves and others to expand, not just in terms of geography, but in terms of consciousness and spirit.

Sisters in Africa will join sisters in Europe, sisters in Asia, sisters in India, sisters in South America, sisters in Canada, sisters in the Caribbean, sisters in the United States, and so on. In fact, Sisterhood Agenda's Global Sisterhood Directory includes resources from all of these countries and sisterhood resources are growing daily.

You can choose to be a part of any sister circle or sisterhood group at any time, privately or publicly. By doing so, you are a part of the global sisterhood movement that teaches, inspires, and empowers. What are you waiting for?

What You Can Do:

- *Think about your comfort level with your heritage. Do you identify strongly with your culture? If so, how so? If not, why not?*

- *Envision a global sisterhood of women joined together for causes in their communities. Think of the causes that are important for females in your community.*

- *Write down the next steps for the future of sisterhood for you and your community.*

REFERENCES

"Wonder Woman."
<http://en.wikipedia.org/wiki/Wonder_Woman>

"The Power of Sister Circles and Safe Spaces."
< http://ourlegaci.com/2013/11/22/the-power-of-sister-circles-and-safe spaces/?goback=%2Egde_3757132_member_58096988062 11584003>

ABOUT

Girls Guide is a how-to book series for inspiration, self-development, and improvement, in the spirit of sisterhood. The book series is a set of resources created by Angela D. Coleman, published by Sisterhood Agenda Enterprises, LLC.

EMAIL

sister@sisterhoodagenda.com

IMAGES

Sisters Forever photograph by Kevin Richards, Kevin Richards Photography. Sati image created by Nancy Danch. Pictures, images, and other photographs are used under public domain unless otherwise noted.

ACKNOWLEDGEMENTS

Thank you, Nancy Danch, for your editing work on this project and your commitment, loving friendship, and support. Thank you to my teachers, especially those who taught me about sisterhood and the significance of being a powerful woman.

Made in the
USA
Middletown, DE